MW01602007

How to Make an Audiobook

For Amazon, iTunes, and Audible

By Tim Morris

Copyright © 2018
All rights reserved.
ISBN: 9781791384418
Published by ZML Corp LLC

Table of Contents

Disclaimer

This book is written for informational and entertainment purposes only. The author and publishing company are not affiliated with any websites, products, or software listed in this book, which includes but is not limited to Amazon, Audible, iTunes, Audacity, and ACX. It is illegal to copy or distribute any part of this book without written consent from the author or publisher. Written by Tim Morris, published by ZML Corp LLC. Copyright © 2019, all rights reserved.

Introduction

In this book I will teach you, from start to finish, everything you need to do to create a stunning audiobook. You will then be able to upload that audiobook to ACX.com, where it will in turn appear on Amazon.com, Audible.com, and in the iTunes store.

I will not just show you how to record the audiobook, but also the equipment and software necessary to make sure the book meets all the standards needed to be ready for upload at ACX.com.

After reading, if you have any questions feel free to contact me at tim@unknownwealth.com. Now let's create our audiobook!

Part 1
Deciding How to Record Your Audiobook

First you need to decide whether or not you want to record the audiobook yourself. You can outsource this process to someone who already has the experience, equipment, a stellar voice, etc. If you have just one book that you plan on really promoting and making big, I would suggest getting a professional to do this for you. The reason for this is the audiobook will most likely sound better. The person you hire will already have all the experience, know how to pitch their voice, edit the files, and it takes the work out of the process for you. This will in turn help you get higher reviews, obtain more sales, etc.

You have a few options for hiring a professional. The first is to go straight to ACX.com. There you will find a large number of book narrators who will record your audiobook for you.

Your second option is outsource to a 3rd party website and find a book narrator there. The 3rd party websites are usually less expensive than ACX.com.

Two websites that are ideal for this are Upwork and Fiverr Shortened links to both sites are below:

fastlink.xyz/upwork | fastlink.xyz/fiver

I would suggest looking around all these sites to find someone with a voice you like, quality reviews, and to see who will do it for the best price. The longer the book, the more you'll pay for a narrating service, due to the fact they will spend more time recording it. For an average sized book, you can expect to pay a few hundred dollars for this service.

If you plan on making multiple audiobooks, don't want to pay someone, or just feel you're the best narrator for your book, recording it yourself is your next option. For all the equipment needed, you can expect to pay a little over $100 for a decent set up. While this is less than hiring a professional, know that your voice and the quality of your audio will most likely not be as "professional" as someone who has a lot of experience narrating. So if this audiobook is a really big deal and you are expecting to make millions from the book you are selling, have a professional do it.

If you have a professional narrate your book for you, you want to make sure they have experience with ACX so they will place the files in the correct format for you to upload them. Read the rest of this book to understand what I'm referring to.

Part 2
Equipment Needed

If you decide to record an audiobook yourself, you'll need to get the proper equipment. The first thing you need to get is a microphone. Microphones range in quality and price, and you can definitely get carried away. There are two types of microphones you can get: a dynamic mic and a condenser mic. I've tried both and in my experience, the condenser mics have been better for audiobook recording. While the dynamic mics have their benefits, such as not picking up as much background noise, they just didn't perform as well as their competitor. There is a quick explainer video on condenser vs. dynamic mics which can be found at this link: **fastlink.xyz/micvideo**

Condenser mics can hook into your computer a few ways: a 3.5mm jack, a USB jack, and a standard 3-pin XLR cable which you convert into USB. Supposedly the last option, the XLR cable, has the best quality however with the converter and mic, your looking at upwards of $500. I've used the straight USB option and found it to be just fine. You'll welcome to look around on your own, however I have found two USB microphones, listed below, which work well for audiobooks. One is a value option and the other is more high end.

The first microphone, the Blue Snowball, goes for $39. The second microphone, the Blue Yeti, goes for $100. You do get what you pay for, so know you will have better quality audio with the Blue Yeti mic. However for most audiobooks, the $39 Blue Snowball works absolutely fine. I have a link below each piece of equipment shown in this book which will take you to the product's page on Amazon.

Blue Snowball USB Microphone

Shortened Link to Amazon Page: **fastlink.xyz/snowball**

Blue Yeti USB Microphone

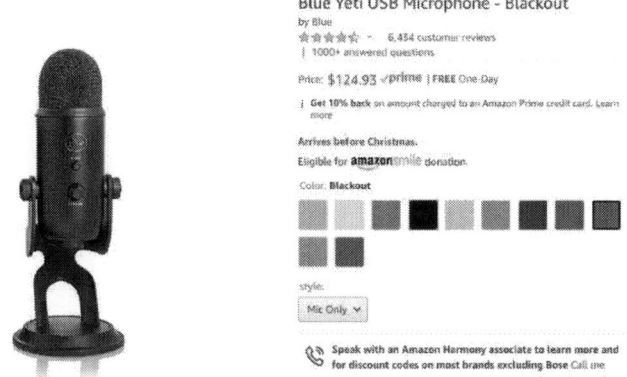

Shortened Link to Amazon Page: **fastlink.xyz/yeti**

After you get a mic, you need to get a pop filter. While they don't look like much, these small filters help tremendously when it comes to filtering out "popping" sounds from your voice. There are quite a few of these on Amazon. The more expensive ones do work better, particularly the Stedman versions. I have two filters below: one is for value, the other is high end ($8 vs. $45).

Aokeo Mesh Pop Filter

Aokeo Professional Microphone Pop Filter Mask Shield, Dual Layered Wind Pop Screen With A Flexible 360° Gooseneck Clip Stabilizing Arm For Awesome Premium Recordings, Broadcasting, Streaming, Singing

by aokeo

★★★★☆ ∨ 161 customer reviews | 29 answered questions

in Microphone Clips

Price: $12.99 ✓prime

Your cost could be $0.00. Eligible customers get a $15 bonus when reloading $100.

Arrives before Christmas.

Eligible for **amazon**smile donation.

Color: **Premium Pop Filter**

Double Layered Screen Pop Filters: The first screen blocks air blasts as any pop filter normally would; The gap in between then disperses any remaining air pressure, so by the time it passes the second screen, the blast is easily contained to produce great quality recordings.

Shortened Link to Amazon Page: **fastlink.xyz/popfilter1**

Stedman PS101 Pop Filter

Stedman PS101

by Stedman

★★★★☆ ∨ 32 customer reviews | 2 answered questions

Price: $46.98 & **FREE Shipping**

Note: Not eligible for Amazon Prime. Available with free Prime shipping from other sellers on Amazon.

- Length: 20"
- Screen diameter: 4.6"
- Clamp opening diameter: .5
- Weight: 5.6 oz.

Compare with similar items

Used & new (18) from $48.98 & FREE shipping

Report incorrect product information.

Enter your child's birthdate for age-based recommendations and more

Birthdate

Shortened Link to Amazon Page: **fastlink.xyz/popfilter2**

While not required, I would also highly recommend obtaining an adjustable stand to place your microphone in. This allows you to have the microphone in a comfortable position as you sit and record the book from your desk. For about $12, it's well worth the price. The one I use and would recommend is below.

InnoGear Mic Stand

InnoGear Microphone Suspension Mic Clip Adjustable Boom Studio Scissor Arm Stand for Blue Yeti Snowball Microphone and Blue Yeti Nano

by InnoGear

★★★★☆ ⌄   773 customer reviews | 90 answered questions

Price: $12.50 ✓prime

Your cost could be $0.00. Eligible customers get a $15 bonus when reloading $100.

Arrives before Christmas.

Eligible for **amazon**smile donation

- Upgraded Desk Mount: Compared with old versions, this zinc alloy desk mount is built with anti-scratch pad and wider mouth up to 2" to fit most desktop.
- The Diameter of Microphone Clip is 1.10". Suitable for any stores, families, stages, studios, broadcasting and TV stations, etc. Attach your Blue Snowball and Blue Yeti with the 5/8"-27 male to 3/8"-16 female threaded screw adapter.
- Note: The mounting hole on the Yeti Mic is sometimes just a tiny fraction bigger than the 5/8" industry standard. Suggestion: Please use Thread Tape (included) to wrap around the mounting screw on your shock mount, effectively increasing the thickness of the mounting screw, while still maintaining the actual screw thread, so you can connect your Yeti.

Compare with similar items

New (3) from $12.50 ✓prime

Shortened Link to Amazon Page: **fastlink.xyz/micstand**

These microphones are very sensitive. Considering the microphone is attached to your desk, it can pick up vibrations from cars outside, your computer fan, etc. For this reason, if you use a mic stand, you want to get what is known as a "shock mount". These mounts use rubber to dampen any vibration that may reach the microphone. Shock mounts are universal, and I have found a great one which works with both the Blue Snowball and Blue Yeti, which I have a picture of and link to below.

Auphonix Shock Mount

Shortened Link to Amazon Page: **fastlink.xyz/shock**

You're going to be listening to your audiobook in the editing process. Most of your customers will be listening with headphones, so I suggest that is the way you listen to it as well. OneOdio has a great pair of headphones on Amazon with excellent sound quality that go for around $35. I have them listed below. While you could use ear buds, the over the ear headphones really immerse you in the audio, and allow you to hear all sounds quite well.

OneOdio Headphones

OneOdio Adapter-Free Closed Back Over-Ear DJ Stereo Monitor Headphones, Professional Studio Monitor & Mixing, Telescopic Arms with Scale, Newest 50mm Neodymium Drivers- Glossy Finish

Shortened Link to Amazon Page:
fastlink.xyz/headphones

For some, background noise may be a problem. Background noise would include the likes of neighbors yelling, air conditioning units running, birds chirping, etc. You may live in a quiet area or be able to record your book at night with no problem. Unfortunately I live in a noisy neighborhood and there is constantly some type of noise outside. If you have a similar problem, you may want to invest in a sound shield. I've used a few different ones, and a problem I had with the larger ones was it was incredibly difficult to use the sound shield while still being able to read my book from the computer screen. This is because the sound shield basically blocked my view of everything around the mic. I have found a sound shield made by Pyle which is small, works effectively, and will not block your view of your computer screen. I have a picture and link to that sound shield below. As stated, this is an important investment if you have any background noise that could get into your audiobooks.

Pyle Sound Shield

Pyle Sound Isolation Recording Booth Shield - 2" Thick Foldable Studio Microphone Dampening Filter Foam Cube, Audio Acoustic Noise Isolator Platform Pads w/ Wedgie Padding, Tripod Base Stand - PSMRS08
by Pyle

★★★★☆ 52 customer reviews | 36 answered questions

Price: $60.99 & **FREE Shipping**. Details & FREE Returns

Free Amazon product support included ∨

- ELIMINATES UNWANTED NOISE: The Foldable Sound Recording Booth Shield features sound dampening foam that blocks unwanted sounds from your recordings. Creates an acoustic boundary around the microphone that improves vocal audio flow
- RECORD LIKE A PRO: Acoustic foam platform pads that block off outside noise such as air conditioning or computer fans, reduce sound reflections or echo and removes unwanted acoustic interference, the soundproof filter will let you record like a pro
- THICK WEDGIE FOAM: Includes 3 high density noise-absorbing wedgie acoustic tiles that promote mic stabilization. Unwanted audio waves and vibrations known as noise and interference, are shielded while your voice has a clear path to your microphone
- ADJUSTABLE ANGLE: The tabletop mic isolator is made portable to easily transport from the studio to the recording booth. With angle, height and depth adjustable panel design for maximum absorption. Perfect for studio recording, podcast, singing

Shortened Link to Amazon Page: **fastlink.xyz/sound**

After you have all your equipment, you have two options for reading your audiobook: read it off your kindle or read it from your computer. If you decide to use your computer, I would highly recommend getting a second screen. Having a second screen makes everything very convenient during the recording process. This is because you can read the book off of one screen while you have the audio recording software running on the other. There is a great screen on Amazon made by Acer that works perfectly for this, and goes for an affordable price. I have a link to that screen below.

Acer 21.5" Monitor

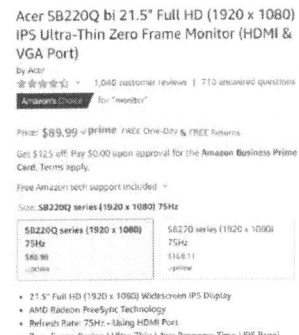

Shortened Link to Amazon Page: **fastlink.xyz/screen**

Most laptops and computers have an HDMI slot which is where you plug in your second screen. Some older screens use a "VGA" cable, however there are converters you can buy to convert the VGA cable into an HDMI plug.

Once the screen is plugged in, most computers recognize it automatically. You may have to go into the settings to show your computer where the screen is located. To do this in Windows, right click on the desktop screen and choose "Display Settings". Then scroll down to where it says "Multiple Displays" to adjust where the screen is located.

Part 3

Audiobook Cover

While you may already have a Kindle book cover, the audiobook cover ACX accepts is a different size. ACX wants their covers to be 2400 x 2400 pixels, as they look like CD covers. Considering you already have a 2D book cover, whoever made it for you can just make you one in the new size.

If this is all new to you and you are making this yourself, you have two other options. The first is to do is yourself with a website called Canva.com. This website is completely free, and allows you to set the dimensions before you make the cover. It provides free graphics, fonts, etc. and makes it much easier, even for the art impaired, to design a cover.

Your second option would be to hire a freelancer. A great, low cost website to do this is called Fiver (**fastlink.xyz/fiver**). This website has many different freelance designers who are willing to make you a high quality audiobook cover for only $6! Many are in foreign countries, however they still speak English and do a great job. When you have your 2D cover created, save this file, and keep it for later when you upload your audiobook to ACX.com.

Part 4

Recording Software

While MacBooks do have a pre-loaded software on them called Garageband, which works fine for this process, I will be going over recording your audiobook with a program called Audacity in this book. Audacity is a free program available for both Windows and Macs. Here is a shortened link to download Audacity:

`fastlink.xyz/audacity`

ACX has certain sound requirements for audiobooks which need to be met or else they won't accept them in their store. For this reason, there are two plugins you have to download, which are used with Audacity, that help your audiobook comply with all ACX guidelines.

ACX Check
`fastlink.xyz/acxcheck`

RMS Normalize
`fastlink.xyz/rms`

Once downloaded, you need to take both files and drag them into the Audacity plug-ins folder. Here is how to find these folders:

On Windows: Go to File Explorer > Local Disk (C:) > Program Files (x86) > Audacity > Plug-Ins

On Mac: Go to Finder > Applications > Audacity > Plug-Ins

After you have placed the plug-in's into their proper folder, you have to activate them in Audacity. To do this, open Audacity. The click Effect, Add/Remove Plug-ins. Find the two plugins you just installed and click the "enable" button. RMS normalize will show under the Effect tab and ACX check will show under the Analyze tab.

Part 5
Recording Your Book

To begin recording your book, you want the microphone to be positioned around 6 inches from your mouth; this provides for the clearest audio. A good way to calculate 6 inches is to make a hang-ten sign with your hand, as shown in the photo below.

Make sure you are in a quiet area without any background noise. Turn off any fans, heaters, etc. that could cause background noise, as the microphone picks up even the faintest noise. Put your cell phone on silent and move both your laptop and cell phone away from the microphone. Both can cause background noise when positioned too close to the microphone.

ACX requires every audiobook to have an "Opening Credits", "Closing Credits", and "Retail Audio Sample".

The opening credits, at a minimum, need to list the book title and subtitle, the author's name, and the narrator's name. So we can start by opening Audacity and creating the "Opening Credits".

Make sure your microphone is plugged in, and Audacity has the correct microphone selected. Most computers default to the built in mic, so you'll need to make sure this isn't the case. The picture below shows you how to choose the correct mic in Audacity.

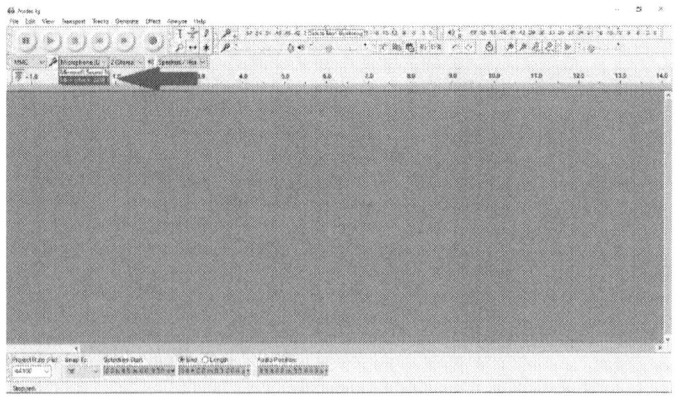

After you have selected the correct mic, change the "stereo" setting to the right of the microphone to "mono". ACX recommends audiobooks be recorded in mono, and not stereo.

Next, you want to adjust the microphone level. I keep the mic level at 90 in Audacity, and turn the "gain" knob on the microphone almost as low as it can go. Having the gain knob too high on your microphone can cause quite a bit of background noise.

Once you're ready, click record and begin narrating your audiobook. Each section of your book has to have at least 0.5-1 second of room tone in the beginning, and 1-5 seconds of room tone at the end. I would suggest letting the recording go for at least 10 seconds when you are done with each chapter, as you will be using this room tone later in the editing process.

If you mess up during your recording, you can either just continue on, repeating the flawed audio and editing it out later, or you click the "stop" button at the top of the screen. If you choose to stop your recording, you can use your mouse to highlight the flawed audio and click "delete" on your keyboard. Then click "Shift+R" on your keyboard. Audacity will immediately start recording at the furthest point of the audio file.

If you just hit "R" on your keyboard, or just click the record button at the top without holding shift, a new audio file opens below the current one, and then you have to combine the two later on. You don't want this hassle, so just make sure to hold "Shift+R" when you begin recording again. ACX.com requires you to upload each chapter separately. For this reason, record each chapter separately on Audacity. When you save the chapters, place a number in front of the file like the example below:

- 01-Opening-Credits
- 02-Chapter-1
- etc.

I will show you the reason for this later in the book. When you are done recording is when the editing happens.

I will show you the reason for this later in the book. When you are done recording is when the editing happens. The first thing you want to do is equalize your audio. Now you will change the equalization settings. You're probably familiar with the bass and treble on your car radio. This is basically what you're changing with equalization, but on a broader scale. Click the effect tab, and then click equalization. When you open up the equalizer, you'll notice it is in a range from 0 hertz (Hz) to 20,000 Hz. From around 1000-2000 Hz is where most human voices lay. Many times room noise and background noise are on the low and high end of this spectrum. For this reason, you want to eliminate everything that is above 16,000 Hz, and below 75 Hz. To do this, click on the line at 75 Hz and drag it down to -60 dB. Then click on the line at 16,000

Hz, and drag it down to -60 dB. It should look like the photo below.

Click the "save/manage curves" button and save this setting. This allows you to instantly use this setting in the future from the "select curve" dropdown, instead of having to manually adjust the curve each time. We'll call this EQ1. Then click "OK" and your noise will equalize.

Next you want to get rid of any background noise. To do this you're going to highlight a small area in the clip where there is no voice. A good place to do this is where you have room tone at the end of your recording.

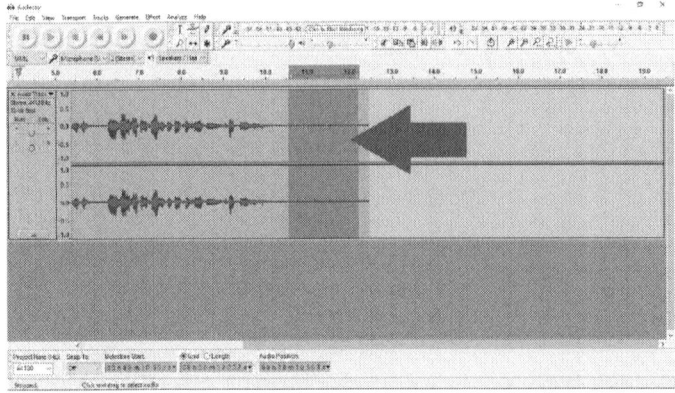

After you highlight an area, click "Effect" at the top of your screen, then "Noise Reduction", then click "Get Noise Profile". Audacity is using the highlighted clip to determine the background noise in your audio file.

The window should close and you will now see your audio file again. Click anywhere on your audio file so it is no longer highlighted. This is important or else the next part won't work.

After you have clicked so your audio file is no longer highlighted, go back to "Effect", then click "Noise Reduction". Next you're going to put the following numbers in:

Noise Reduction (dB): 30
Sensitivity: 15.00
Frequency Smoothing (bands): 4

You may need to adjust these numbers a little to your liking, but overall, these settings have worked well for me. Then you will click "OK" at the bottom. This will remove all background noise from your audio file. In terms of what these settings mean, here is the text directly from the Audacity Team website.

Noise Reduction: Controls the amount of volume reduction to be applied to the identified noise. Use the lowest value that reduces the noise to an acceptable level. Higher values than necessary may make the noise even quieter, but will result in damage to the audio that remains

Sensitivity: Controls how much of the audio will be considered as noise, on a scale of 0 (off) to 24 (maximum). Greater sensitivity means that more noise will be removed, possibly at the expense of removing some of the desired signal as well. Lower values may result in the appearance of artifacts in the noise-reduced audio. Set this control to the lowest value that achieves effective noise removal without the introduction of artifacts.

Frequency Smoothing (bands): At values of 1 or higher, this control spreads the noise reduction into the specified number of neighboring bands. This modifies the signal you were intending to keep, but if artifacts remain in the noise-reduced audio the smoothing can make those artifacts sound more acceptable. There is a chance that smoothing will make the desired audio less clear, so where your desired signal is strong and of wide frequency range and the noise is light, try leaving this control at 0 (off).

When equalization is completed, you want to amplify your audio file. This will normalize the sound, making it louder. To do this click the effect tab, and then click amplify. Set the "new peak amplitude", which is the bottom number, to 0. This will change the top number automatically. Then click OK. Now we will compress the file. Audio compression helps to make audio file more equal, in that it increases quieter parts of your audio, while reducing louder parts. The compression settings I use are below. They have worked well for me, however feel free to learn more about compression on your own and tweak these to your liking. Click the effect tab, then click compressor.

Threshold: -30 dB
Noise Floor: -60 dB
Ratio: 3:1
Attack Time: 0.10 sec
Release Time: 1 sec

After you have compressed your audio, it is now time to normalize the sound, making it the appropriate level for ACX. To do this, we will be using the RMS Normalize plugin we downloaded earlier. Click effect, RMS Normalize (it's down near the bottom). Then set the following:

Target RMS Level: -20.00 dB

ACX accepts an RMS level between -18db and -23db, so -20db is right in the middle. If you don't see "RMS Normalize" in the "Effect" menu, make sure you have placed the "RMS" plug-in we downloaded at the beginning of this book in the Audacity plug-in folder, and then enabled it in Audacity. You may need to restart Audacity or even restart your computer for it to show correctly. Once this is done we will now adjust our "Limiter". There are certain audio peaks which ACX does not accept, so what the limiter does it clip these peaks so they don't go over the dB threshold. To set the limiter, go to "Effect", "Limiter", then put in these settings:

Type: Hard Limit
Input Gain Right/Left Channel: 0.00
Limit to (dB): -7.00
Hold (ms): 10.00
Apply Make-Up Gain: No

The "Limit to (dB)" is what matters most here. I personally like limiting my audio file more, as it makes the overall tone more equal.

You may not have to do this next step, however with a Blue Yeti mic and the gain turned all the way down, I do. We are going to be performing another equalization and noise reduction. When you amplified and compressed the sound, it most likely brought up some of the quieter background noise that wasn't audible before. This creates buzzing in the background when the volume is turned high, which does not sound pleasant. First perform an equalization by bringing up the curve you had saved before (EQ1). You can do this by clicking "Effect", "Equalization", and then finding it in the dropdown list. Then click okay and it will equalize the noise.

Next perform that 2nd noise reduction by repeating the steps that allowed us to do a noise reduction before. As in highlight a section of audio with just background noise, then click "Effect," "Noise Reduction," "Get Noise Profile." Then click anywhere so your audio is no longer highlighted. Then again click "Effect,"

"Noise Reduction," and use the same number settings we used previously and click "OK."

Many people talk a little too fast when recording a book, and listeners prefer a slower speed. Luckily, there is a feature in Audacity to help with this. You are able change the audio tempo in Audacity to make the audio a little easier to listen to for your customers. To do this go to "Effect", then "Change Tempo". I usually slow down the tempo by -2%, however you may want to play with this depending on how slow or fast you talk.

If you don't like how slow or fast it is after you change the tempo, just click "Edit", then "Undo Change Tempo", or click Ctrl-Z on your keyboard. Then repeat the process until you find a speed you like.

After this is done, you're going to take out breath sounds and audio imperfections (mouse clicks, tapping, etc.). The picture on the next page has an arrow pointed to what breath sounds look like it Audacity.

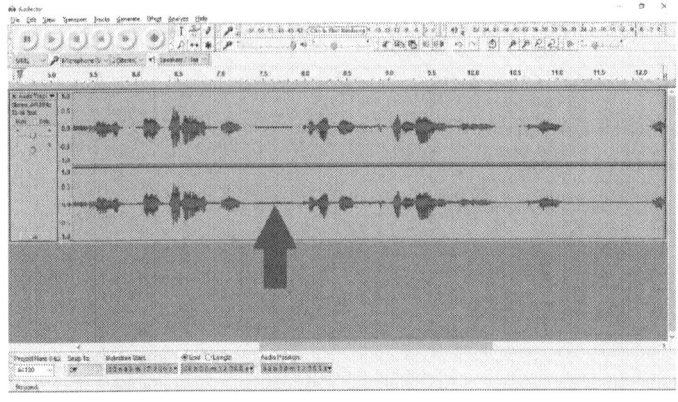

As you can see, they look like little blue blips in between your actual vocals. When you listen to your voice recordings, it will sound much better when this is done. Be careful to just get the breathe sounds, and not any of your actual voice recording. Sometimes you may hear a breath sound without seeing a blue blip. This is because it's quieter. To get a better view, magnify your audio file. To do this left click on your mouse on the "0.0" number on the far left of the audio file. Many times the breath will become visible when you do this. Some authors leave breath sounds in sentences, and just take them out in between paragraphs. I personally try to take them out everywhere unless removing it affects the flow of the audio file.

Editing your audio book is time consuming, they say for every one hour you record, you should allocate 7 hours to editing. While I don't spend this much time, it still takes a while. However editing is very important and will greatly improve the quality of your audio, so it's needed.

After you have taken out all breathe sounds and audio imperfections in between your vocals, you want to listen to your entire voice recording. Sometimes there are faint sounds that are not shown in the visuals, which you'll want to remove if you hear them. You also want to delete any gaps in between sentences that should connect with each other. To do this, just highlight the gapped area, and click the "delete" button on your keyboard.

If you want to place silence in between your spoken words, do NOT use the "silence" feature on Audacity. While it will silence your audio, it takes away from the flow of your audiobook and sounds choppy. Instead, you're going to use room tone. As mentioned before, you left at least 10 seconds of room tone at the end of your audio file. You can take a small section of it and copy it onto your clipboard. You can then paste this room tone audio anywhere that you need it.

After everything is complete and you are satisfied with your recording, you can now check if it is properly formatted for ACX (which it will be if you followed all the instructions up to this point). To do this, we will be using the "ACX Check" plugin we downloaded before. At the top of the screen click the "Analyze" tab, then "ACX Check", and it will automatically start examining your audio to make sure it complies with ACX guidelines. Once complete, it should display a pop-up which reads "Clip Meets ACX Requirements". If it displays an error, you have to fix this issue before you try uploading it to the ACX store. Unfortunately I cannot go over all the possible errors, however a quick Google search with the error code should help you solve your issue.

Now is a good time to listen to your recording again and verify everything sounds okay. You want to make sure there are no odd noises in the clip, you've taken out all the breath sounds, and everything is to your liking. Once this is done, you now have to convert the Audacity file into an MP3 file. To do this go to "File", "Export-Audio". When you click export, there is a drop-down menu which allows you to set the file quality. You have to set this to 192 kbps for it to be acceptable to ACX. I would suggest saving your files with a number in the front as shown below:

- 01-OpeningCredits.mp3
- 02-Chapter1.mp3
- etc.

The reason for this is they will save in the correct order, which will make it easier for you to upload them onto ACX.com. Also, as shown in the next section, if you need to make changes to the book in the future, it will be in the format ACX accepts.

Know also that ACX requires three additional files which you may not be aware of. They include:

- The Opening Credits
- The Closing Credits
- Retail Audio Sample

The opening credits will be the first audio file in your list. ACX requires that the opening credits include:

- The Title/Subtitle of the Book
- The Author of The Book
- The Narrator of the Book

The closing credits will be the second to last file in your list. At a minimum, the closing credits need to include the words "The End". The third required file is the retail audio sample. This is the sample that the customer can listen to when they view your book on Audible, Amazon, or iTunes, and will help them determine if they want to buy your book. This retail audio sample can be a big deal, because if the customer doesn't like how the audio sounds or the information they hear, they most likely will not buy your book. I would suggest using a section of your book that will draw the customer in, and then leave them hanging so they want more! The retail audio sample has a length limit of 5 minutes, so you may need to trim it down if the audio file you copy is longer than that.

As a token of appreciation to my readers, I am offering the special report above titled *Amazon Advertising Secrets* **absolutely free**. In this report, you'll learn a unique marketing strategy which will greatly accelerate your Kindle and audiobook sales! Just copy & paste the link below into your browser and put in your email address, and it will immediately be sent to you!

fastlink.xyz/secrets

Part 6

How to Upload Book to ACX.com

You're going to go to ACX.com and sign in. This website uses the same login as your Amazon account. Then click "Add Your Title" in the top right corner of the screen.

You will then need to search for your book in the Kindle store. You can do this by typing in the author name or the title of the book. When you find it, click "This is My Book", and then click "I already have audio files for this book, and I want to sell it". Then you will agree to the ACX terms of use, and start the uploading process.

Take your saved MP3 files, and upload them individually, making sure to properly title each chapter after you upload it. The title you put down will be what displays when customers listen to your audiobook, so you don't want it titled something like "04-file2.mp3". Make sure to include the opening credits, closing credits, and retail audio sample. When this is complete, you'll be able to upload your audiobook cover.

After the audiobook cover is uploaded, you'll write a description for your audiobook. For this I would just use a similar description to the one you have in the Kindle store. Just know that ACX has a character limit of 2,000 characters in their description, which includes spaces. They also don't accept HTML editing.

After all this is done, ACX has to verify your audiobook meets all their guidelines. The entire process takes quite some time, as in up to 14 business days, sometimes longer. And if your book doesn't meet their guidelines, then you have to re-do your files and start this process all over again. For this reason, it's very important to run that ACX check plugin on Audacity before you submit your files to ACX.com, so you only have to complete this whole process once.

Once ACX accepts your audiobook and it's displayed in the Audible store, it can take a few days before it shows as linked to your Kindle book on Amazon. If after a few days it's still not linked, you can email support@acx.com and they will be able to help you.

After all is said and done, your audiobook will be available for purchase on Audible.com, Amazon.com, and in the iTunes store.

Part 7

How to Update Book After Submitted

If you ever make a new version of your book, or want to submit a new version of your audiobook for any reason, the process is a little different. First, save the MP3 files with the numbers in front (as stated before). Make sure your "Opening Credit" file is first, your "Closing Credits" file is last. Place all your files into a zipped folder and go to the ACX Hightail Dropbox (shortened link below).

```
fastlink.xyz/acxdrop
```

You will then drag the zipped folder into the "dropbox". After that, email support@acx.com to tell them you have re-submitted your audiobook and include the book title and author name in your email. They will get it re-uploaded for you within 7-10 business days.

If you want to update the "Retail Audio Sample" and not the actual book, you have to e-mail support@acx.com with the book name, author, and attached MP3 file. Unfortunately this is a separate process.

Conclusion

I hope I was able to help guide you effectively on making an audiobook. If you have any questions, feel free to email me at tim@unknownwealth.com.

If you found value in this book, please leave a review on Amazon. It is greatly appreciated! A shortened link to the review page is below:

fastlink.xyz/audiobook

If you found this book helpful, you may also enjoy:

How to Make a Kindle and Paperback Book on Amazon

Shortened Link to Amazon Page:
fastlink.xyz/makebook

Amazon has made becoming an author easier than ever! Now you too can make a Kindle & paperback book & have it selling within 24 hours! In this book, Tim Morris shows you exactly how to go from your rough draft to your finished, uploaded product. It's the smoothest guide out there on how to make a book. Find out more at the link above!

Unknown Wealth

The Quickest, Easiest Way to Become Rich Online

Shortened Link to Amazon Page:
fastlink.xyz/wealth

Tim Morris shows you the secrets the top gurus in the field have been using for years to acquire wealth online. Tim holds nothing back and provides you with all the secrets that you too can use to become rich using the internet. Whether you want to make a little money on the side, or start a full time business, it all can be done with the strategies provided in this book

Made in the USA
Middletown, DE
06 November 2019